\ \

The Progressive Movement 1900–1920
Efforts to Reform America's New Industrial Society ™

THE MUCKRAKERS

American Journalism During the Age of Reform

Aileen Gallagher

rosen central
Primary Source ™

The Rosen Publishing Group, Inc., New York

For Syracuse University professors Charlotte Grimes and Joel Kaplan, who taught me about the rake, and the staff of The Daily Orange, *who let me practice using it.*

Published in 2006 by The Rosen Publishing Group, Inc.
29 East 21st Street, New York, NY 10010

First Edition

Library of Congress Cataloging-in-Publication Data

Gallagher, Aileen.
The Muckrakers: American journalism during the age of reform / Aileen Gallagher.
    p. cm.—(The progressive movement, 1900-1920: efforts to reform America's new industrial society)
Includes bibliographical references and index.
ISBN 1-4042-0197-1 (lib. bdg.)
ISBN 1-4042-0865-8 (pbk. bdg.)
6-pack ISBN 1-4042-6190-7
1. Journalism—Social aspects—United States—History—20th century. 2. Social problems—Press coverage—United States. 3. United States—Social conditions—20th century.
I. Title. II. Series.
PN4888.S6G35 2004
302.23'0973'09042—dc22
                                                                        2004002683

Manufactured in the United States of America

On the cover: Top: American novelist and muckraker Upton Sinclair (1878–1968), known for exposing the mistreatment of immigrant meatpackers in nineteenth-century Chicago. Bottom: A photograph of a Chicago stockyard in 1900.

Photo Credits: Cover (top) Hulton/Archive/Getty Images; cover (bottom), pp. 5 (left), 7, 10, 14, 21, 25, 26 Library of Congress Prints and Photographs Division; p. 5 (inset) © Museum of the City of New York; p. 11 Historic Newspaper Archives; p. 11(top) Roosevelt Island, www.nyc10044.com; pp. 16 (left), 19 Courtesy of The Ida M. Tarbell Collection, Special Collections, Pelletier Library, Allegheny College; p. 16 (right) Brown Brothers; p. 24 Bildarchiv Preussischer Kulturbesitz, Berlin.

Designer: Les Kanturek; Editor: Joann Jovinelly; Photo Researcher: Amy Feinberg

Contents

Chapter One

Exposing the Truth

T he United States grew at such a rapid pace during the Industrial Revolution that the country experienced growing pains. A sharp rise in population, corrupt business and political practices, and social injustice led to a turn-of-the-century reform movement known as the Progressive Era (c. 1900–1920). Some of the greatest contributors of this era of reform were investigative journalists known as muckrakers.

Earlier, in 1890, many people across America read a book called *How the Other Half Lives*. It told the story of the poor who packed the tenement slums of New York City. Americans did not know anything about these tenements, which were small, dark, and often windowless apartments. The tenements were originally built for single families, but New York's growing population needed places to live. Soon, tenement apartments were divided into smaller units that

Jacob August Riis (1849–1914), the writer, photographer, and social activist, is pictured in this 1904 portrait alongside his famous book about the slums in nineteenth-century New York City. *How the Other Half Lives*, seen in this 1892 edition, drew national attention to the poor conditions in New York's tenement dwellings and the hardships faced by European and Asian immigrants.

housed many families. Americans did not know that these crowded apartments often made people sick.

The man who wrote *How the Other Half Lives* was named Jacob Riis. Riis came to New York from Denmark in 1870, when he was twenty-one years old. Riis was poor when he came to New York. He learned English and became a crime reporter for the *New York Tribune*. Riis wrote about murders and robberies in the slums. The poverty and filth he saw there made Riis sad and angry. He believed that if other people could witness

The Progressive Movement

The Progressive movement in America happened roughly between 1900 and 1920. During this period, progress in the country was made in the form of new laws. Over time, America became a better place to live and work. New legislation helped immigrants and the poor. Many ideas for the reforms came from wealthy Americans. They believed the country should be a better place for everyone. Many Progressives had strong religious beliefs, which included helping those people who were less fortunate. After World War I (1914–1918), many Americans lost interest in the Progressive movement. They thought instead about issues facing the world, not just the United States.

Immigrant families like this one often lived in dark, dank tenement rooms with little sunlight and poor air circulation. Jacob A. Riis took this photograph in 1889, while writing about the substandard living conditions of New York's Lower East Side residents.

these conditions, then they would be angry enough to help improve them.

Things began to change after people learned about the slums. New tenement buildings were bigger. They had more light and fresh air. Children could play in playgrounds instead of in the streets. *How the Other Half Lives* made people recognize inadequate conditions and work to reform them. In 1890, Riis wrote another book about impoverished children in New York City called *The Children of the Poor*.

Riis and other writers like him were called muckrakers because they "dug" up the truth, or muck. In 1906, President Theodore Roosevelt said writers like Riis only saw the muck, or the bad things in life. Still, the muckrakers were proud of their accomplishments. They knew people's lives could be made better if the rest of America knew the truth about urban poverty.

After *How the Other Half Lives* was published, other writers began to expose society's ills, too. They wrote about children who went to work instead of to school. They wrote about companies that broke laws. And they wrote about rotten things in food that made people sick.

People read articles and books by the muckrakers and wanted things to change. The muckrakers were one group who worked to improve living and working conditions for all Americans during the Progressive movement. Often, people in power also learned about situations that needed improvement by reading the muckrakers' articles.

Chapter Two

Going Undercover

Editors at the *Pittsburgh Dispatch* received a letter in 1885 from an eighteen-year-old named Elizabeth Cochrane. However, because it was so well written, they believed that a man must have authored it. Later, Cochrane wrote her articles under the name Nellie Bly. The name came from a popular song of the day.

The woman known as Bly found plenty of stories to tell in Pittsburgh. Her first story for the *Dispatch* was about divorced women. Although few women were divorced in the 1880s, many of those who were found themselves poor and caring for children.

Next, Bly decided to write about a textile factory. However, she didn't just visit the factory. Bly got the story by working there. She wanted to know what working in a factory was really like. Today, reporters call this style of investigation "going undercover." In the factory, Bly met

Elizabeth Cochrane (1867–1922), more often remembered by her pen name Nellie Bly, was one of the first female newspaper journalists to write about serious issues of the era, such as the unfit environment in mental hospitals, factory sweatshops, and jails.

girls who should have been in school. Instead, they worked to help support their families. The girls had to squint to see what they were doing because the light in the factory was so poor. Few of them could afford to buy glasses. In some cases, the girls' eyesight worsened because of such conditions.

Bly moved to New York in May 1887. Although she visited every newspaper in the city, none of them would hire women. Bly sneaked into the office of Joseph Pulitzer, the publisher of the *New York World*. At the time, the *World* was the biggest newspaper in New York. Bly told Pulitzer her new idea for a story: she wanted to go undercover at a mental hospital to learn what living conditions were like for the mentally ill.

To get her story, Bly pretended to be insane in September 1887, and city workers believed her. She was sent to the

In 1887, Bly exposed the inappropriate conditions in New York's mental hospital on Blackwell's Island *(top)* in an article written for Joseph Pulitzer's *New York World (bottom)*. The article, along with a book about her experiences, *Ten Days in a Mad-House* (1887), prompted a grand-jury investigation into the medical care of mental patients in the nineteenth century.

Blackwell's Island

The insane asylum was not the only scary place on Blackwell's Island. Although the island is less than 2 miles (3.21 km) long, it also contained a jail and a workhouse. In the nineteenth century, people arrested for small crimes often spent a few days in the workhouse. There was also a poorhouse on the island for people who could not afford a place to live. The island's name was changed to Welfare Island in 1921. In 1973, the city renamed the island again. This time it was called Roosevelt Island. Today it is home to nearly 10,000 New Yorkers.

Women's Lunatic Asylum on Blackwell's Island (present-day Roosevelt Island). Inside the asylum were women who were physically ill, illiterate, and poor. Although few of the women were insane, the hospital would not release them.

Bly spent ten days on Blackwell's Island before representatives from the *New York World* could get her released. However, her stories made people in New York pay attention to Blackwell's asylum. Hundreds wrote letters to the *World*, demanding something be done to help the women. The city took notice too. Bly's articles sparked a city investigation of activities on Blackwell's Island. A muckraker had changed things again.

Chapter Three

The First Muckraker

Although Lincoln Steffens's work was published after Jacob Riis's and Nellie Bly's, he is remembered as the first muckraker. He is certainly one of the most famous. In October 1902, *McClure's Magazine* published Steffens's article "Tweed Days in St. Louis." The article profiled corrupt leaders in St. Louis. The people who ran the government in the city were stealing money from its citizens.

Steffens wrote "The Shame of Minneapolis" in January 1903. This article was also about corruption. Politicians in Minneapolis were powerful, but they also used their power to steal. No one knew about the thievery until Steffens wrote about it.

Steffens was a reporter and editor for New York newspapers before joining *McClure's*. One of his friends was President Theodore Roosevelt. Steffens tried to reform

THE "BRAINS"

This nineteenth-century political cartoon by Thomas Nast illustrates another way in which muckrakers exposed corruption. By depicting New York's politician William M. "Boss" Tweed with a bag of money as his head, Nast mocked the corrupt Tweed administration in 1871. Even immigrants who couldn't read English became aware of Tweed's financial gains resulting from fraud and tax favors.

New York. He wanted the people who ran the city to obey its laws. He wanted politicians who were elected honestly and who would not steal from the city.

Steffens spent his first four months as an editor of *McClure's* sitting behind a desk. He was bored. Steffens's boss

Michael Moore, Modern Muckraker

The most famous muckrakers wrote during the Progressive movement, but there are still muckrakers today. One of them is a writer and filmmaker named Michael Moore. Moore became famous for making a documentary called *Roger & Me*. The movie is about the economic hardships faced by people living in Moore's hometown of Flint, Michigan. Most people in Flint worked for General Motors. However, when General Motors closed the factory, Flint became an impoverished city. Moore's movie taught people about the costs of moving American business out of the country. His 2002 movie about guns in America, *Bowling for Columbine*, won an Oscar for best documentary of the year.

told him to go out and find a story. Steffens remembered the corruption in New York. Because he thought other cities might have the same problem, he visited St. Louis, Missouri, and Minneapolis, Minnesota, to unearth unfair practices in those cities, too.

Steffens's stories were so popular they were collected in a book called *Shame of the Cities*. He also wrote about Pittsburgh and Philadelphia, Pennsylvania, and Chicago, Illinois. Other cities invited Steffens to examine their governments. Although *Shame of the Cities* did not make

McClure's Magazine

VOL. XX   *JANUARY, 1903*   NO. 3

THE SHAME OF MINNEAPOLIS

The Rescue and Redemption of a City that was Sold Out

BY LINCOLN STEFFENS

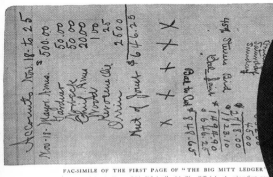

FAC-SIMILE OF THE FIRST PAGE OF "THE BIG MITT LEDGER"

An account kept by a swindler of the dealings of his "Joint" with City Officials, showing first pay... Ames, his brother, the Chief of Police and Detectives. This book figured in trials and newspaper rep... but was "lost"; and its whereabouts was the mystery of the proceedings. This is the first glimp... cept "Cheerful Charlie" Howard, who kept it, and members of the grand jury, has had of the book...

WHENEVER anything extraordinary is done in American municipal politics, whether for good or for evil, you can trace it almost invariably to one man. The people do not do it. Neither do the "gangs," "combines," or political parties. These are but instruments by which bosses (not leaders; we Americans are not led, but driven) rule the people, and commonly sell them out. But there are at least two forms of the autocracy which has supplanted the democracy here as it has everywhere it has been tried. One is that of the organized majority by which, as in Tammany Hall in New York and the Republican machine in Philadelphia, the boss has normal control of more than half the voters. The other is that of the ... managed minority. The "good people" ... herded into parties and stupefied with co... victions and a name, Republican or Democrat; while the "bad people" are so organized or interested by the boss that he can wield their votes to enforce terms with party managers and decide elections. St. Louis is a conspicuous example of this form. Minneapolis is another. Colonel Ed. Butler is the unscrupulous opportunist who handled the non-partisan minority which turned St. Louis into a "boodle town." In Minneapolis "Doc" Ames was the man.

Lincoln Steffens (1866–1936, *right*) was among those writers referred to as muckrakers by President Theodore Roosevelt. Steffens became managing editor of *McClure's Magazine (left)* in 1901, where he published many articles about the political corruption in America's cities. His compiled articles became his most famous work, *Shame of the Cities* (1906).

governments pass new laws or cause bad leaders to resign, it did make voters furious. Many of them never knew that their votes were stolen. Others were shocked that politicians only hired their friends for city jobs.

Sometimes the truths muckrakers exposed did not immediately change laws. More often than not, the muckrakers' stories changed people's minds. Citizens who read *Shame of the Cities* wanted new leaders. They wanted every vote counted. People wanted jobs to go to the most qualified people, not an official's friends. Voters spoke at the ballot box. They elected new, honest leaders.

Steffens's reporting made muckraking famous. His articles inspired other writers. Readers wanted to learn about other problems in their country. The nation was ready for change. Magazines and newspapers were suddenly filled with stories like Steffens's. Muckrakers examined everything. Later muckrakers wrote about greedy corporations. Others investigated race relations, child labor, the pharmaceutical industry, and how food goes from the farm to the dinner table.

Chapter Four

Tackling Unfair Business Practices

In the 1890s, a magazine editor named S. S. McClure read an article written by Ida M. Tarbell. McClure liked the article so much that he went to visit Tarbell at her home in Paris, France. While in Paris, he asked her to write for his magazine, *McClure's*, a publication known for publishing muckraking articles.

Tarbell and her assistant, John Siddall, worked for two years on a story about Standard Oil Company. It took two years because Tarbell wanted to know everything she could about Standard Oil. She learned about the leadership and hard work that make a company great. However, she also learned how Standard Oil stole from and bribed its clients.

Tarbell did not accuse Standard Oil of breaking the law. She did not tell her readers that the company practiced bad business. Tarbell only told the story of Standard Oil

ULY 1905   PRICE TEN CENTS

M^CCLURE'S MAGAZINE

JOHN D ROCKEFELLER
A CHARACTER SKETCH BY IDA M. TARBELL

Ida Minerva Tarbell (1857–1944, *right*), another muckraking journalist who worked at *McClure's Magazine* from 1894 to 1906, is best remembered for her serialized articles that traced the rise and fall of John D. Rockefeller's Standard Oil Company *(left)*.

and let people make up their own minds. Tarbell's first article about Standard Oil was published in *McClure's* in November 1902. It took until 1904 and nineteen articles for Tarbell to tell the whole story.

John D. Rockefeller founded Standard Oil. He was once the richest man in America. Standard Oil made 97 percent

John D. Rockefeller

John Davison Rockefeller was born on July 8, 1839. Rockefeller saved $1,000 in 1859 to start a company with a friend. In 1870, Rockefeller took the money he had made and started Standard Oil. People were using kerosene to light their homes and needed to buy oil for the lamps. By 1882, Standard Oil was worth $70 million. Rockefeller believed in giving his money away to charity. His donations started the University of Chicago. The Rockefeller Foundation still exists today. It provides money for projects from scientific research to the arts. Rockefeller donated more than $540 million during his life.

of the nation's oil in the late 1890s. The government allowed Standard Oil to run its business however it wanted. A law called the Sherman Antitrust Act was created to keep big businesses from becoming too powerful. However, the Sherman Antitrust law was ineffective because it was not fully enforced. The owners of big businesses paid the least attention of all.

Standard Oil's executives tried to put their competitors out of business and blocked new businesses from opening. The executives threatened or blackmailed competitors. Standard Oil's leaders asked the government not to make tougher laws so they would not have to

This political cartoon illustrates the far-reaching effects of Rockefeller's Standard Oil Company by showing one of its oil tanks as an octopus. Its tentacles are wrapped around the steel, copper, and shipping industries, as well as the state house, the U.S. Capitol, and the White House. The Standard Oil monopoly was broken up in 1911 under the Sherman Antitrust Act.

change the way they did business. Standard Oil was a monopoly. A monopoly is a company that controls an entire industry, like electricity or railroads.

After Tarbell told the story of Standard Oil, the government passed and enforced laws that were more strict. In 1914, President Woodrow Wilson signed the Clayton Antitrust Act. This law strengthened the Sherman Antitrust

Act. The Clayton Antitrust Act made price discrimination illegal. Before Clayton, companies could charge two customers different prices for the same product or service. The law also allowed unions to go on strike. Workers could help themselves instead of hoping a muckraker would notice and write about them.

Standard Oil did not survive Tarbell's story. The United States Supreme Court forced Standard Oil to break up into smaller companies beginning in 1911. After the breakup, a variety of companies provided the nation's oil, not only one.

Chapter Five

The Jungle

Before the Industrial Revolution, Americans often grew their own food. However, people living in cities had to buy their food and did not know where it came from. After reading a book by Upton Sinclair called *The Jungle*, people became more informed about food production in America.

Sinclair was a young reporter for a political newspaper named *Appeal to Reason*. The newspaper sent Sinclair to Chicago to investigate its stockyards. Most of America's cattle went through the Chicago stockyards on the way to the slaughterhouse.

Sinclair thought his story would be about the people who worked in the stockyards. It was the summer of 1904 and the workers were on strike. Sinclair found the story of the meat production more interesting than the tale of the workers for good reason. The federal government did

The most famous of all the muckraking journalists was Upton Sinclair (1878–1968), seen here in 1930. During the time he was employed at New York's Socialist weekly *Appeal to Reason*, Sinclair went to Chicago to investigate the mistreatment of immigrant meatpackers. The article eventually became the bestseller *The Jungle*.

not pay attention to food production. There were no rules about food preparation, especially about the safe handling of beef. Cows that were sick were not separated from the rest of the cattle line. Waste, hair, and bone sometimes ended up in hamburger meat. Spoiled food could be sold in the market.

This nineteenth-century lithograph advertises Upton Sinclair's book, *The Jungle*, which exposed the mistreatment of meatpackers and the impurities in processed meat. The meatpacking industry, which was unregulated before Sinclair's best-selling exposé, soon fell under the control of new legislation, including the Pure Food and Drug Act (1906).

Conditions for the stockyard employees were also miserable. Some workers spent their entire day standing in pools of blood. Injuries were common because workers used sharp knives on the cow carcasses. Occasionally, the workers were even killed.

Like Jacob Riis, Sinclair was a voice for those who had none. The stockyard workers were mostly poor immigrants. Wealthy Americans knew nothing about the stockyards until Sinclair wrote the story.

The Jungle was first published in *Appeal to Reason* in 1905. In 1906, it was published as a book. *The Jungle*

Cattle are being stunned in this photograph taken at a Chicago stockyard in 1900. Thanks to writers like Upton Sinclair, citizens of the United States were made aware of the mistreatment of workers and animals in the U.S. meatpacking industry. Within a few years of *The Jungle*'s success, the Meat Inspection Act (1906) improved the safety of meatpackers and the treatment of cattle.

Wholesome Meat Act of 1967

Upton Sinclair was invited to the White House in 1967. President Lyndon B. Johnson asked Sinclair to be there when Johnson signed the Wholesome Meat Act. The act improved the existing Pure Food and Drug Act of 1906. Although Sinclair wrote *The Jungle* in 1904, citizens and the government were still concerned about food safety. People continued to read *The Jungle* and wonder about their food. The Wholesome Meat Act made sure that states had the same meat safety rules as the federal government. Now everyone, everywhere, had to follow the same laws. Food was made safer throughout the United States. What Sinclair had written 60 years before still caused positive change.

Even with updated laws, meat production is still dangerous. In 2001, Eric Schlosser wrote *Fast Food Nation*, a modern examination of the meat industry. Schlosser found that meatpacking plants were still dangerous places to work. Sick cows were still sent to the slaughterhouse with healthy cows. Both ended up on the dinner table. Schlosser's book raised peoples' awareness. Some readers said they would never eat beef again. The book pressured fast food restaurants to make their food safer for consumers. Schlosser's book is a modern piece of muckraking journalism. *Fast Food Nation* informed a new generation of readers about the need for improved food safety.

scared Americans. Some people swore never to eat beef again. Others demanded the government's help.

In 1905, the government was not used to watching what its citizens ate. People cried out for better laws. The government listened and passed the Pure Food and Drug Act and the Meat Inspection Act in 1906. Now food and drugs were to be labeled. Consumers would know exactly what they were eating. They would know what was in the pills they swallowed.

Muckrakers helped make America safer and better for its people. Although the Progressive movement has ended, journalists still rake the muck. Contemporary muckrakers still write about children, the poor, disease, and greedy business practices. As long as the world has problems, muckrakers will continue to write about and expose them to affect positive reforms.

afford (uh-FORD) To be able to pay for.

asylum (uh-SY-lum) A hospital for people who are mentally or physically ill.

corruption (kor-UP-shun) An abuse of power.

immigrant (IH-muh-grint) A person who moves to one country from another.

monopoly (muh-NAH-puh-lee) A company that eliminates competition in order to control an entire industry.

reform (rih-FORM) To improve, to make better.

stockyard (STOK-yard) A large pen where pigs or cattle are kept before slaughter.

strike (STRYK) When workers stop working to get higher wages.

tenement (TEN-uh-ment) A crowded, rundown apartment building.

textiles (TEK-stylz) Clothing and fabrics.

Due to the changing nature of Internet links, the Rosen Publishing Group, Inc., has developed an online list of Web sites related to the subject of this book. This site is updated regularly. Please use this link to access the list:

http://www.rosenlinks.com/pmnhnt/muck

Primary Source Image List

Page 5: Writer, photographer, and activist Jacob A. Riis in a portrait by Pach Brothers in 1904. It is now housed at the U.S. Library of Congress in Washington, D.C. Riis is pictured beside a photograph of the 1892 edition of his most famous work, *How the Other Half Lives*, currently housed in the Museum of the City of New York.

Page 7: Jacob A. Riis took this photograph of an immigrant family living in New York in 1889. The image is now part of the permanent collection of the U.S. Library of Congress in Washington, D.C.

Page 10: This three-quarter length portrait of journalist Nellie Bly (Elizabeth Cochrane) was taken by H. J. Myers in 1890. It is now housed at the U.S. Library of Congress in Washington, D.C.

Page 11 (top): *The Women in the Yard at the Asylum* was originally published in *Harper's Weekly*. From the collection of *The Main Street WIRE*.

Page 11 (bottom): The October 9, 1887, edition of the *New York World* featuring the undercover article by Nellie Bly and the headline, "Behind Asylum Bars: The Mystery of the Unknown Insane Girl."

Page 14: This illustration of Tammany Hall leader William M. "Boss" Tweed with a bag of money as his head was drawn by Thomas Nast for *Harper's Weekly* in 1871.

Page 16 (left): This January 1903 *McClure's Magazine* article is from Special Collections, Pelletier Library, Allegheny College, Meadville, Pennsylvania.

Page 16 (right): An undated photograph of Lincoln Steffens from the Brown Brothers collection.

Page 19: Ida Minerva Tarbell (right) is shown in an undated, unsigned portrait alongside one of her serialized articles (left) describing the life of John D. Rockefeller and the history of his Standard Oil Company. Both images are from The Ida M. Tarbell Collection, Special Collections, Pelletier Library, Allegheny College, Meadville, Pennsylvania.

Page 21: Udo J. Keppler created this political cartoon in September 1904. It is now housed as part of the Periodical Illustrations Collection of the U.S. Library of Congress in Washington, D.C.

Page 24: Erich Salomon took this photograph of Upton Sinclair in Hollywood, California, in 1930.

Page 25: An unknown artist created this lithograph to advertise *The Jungle* in 1906. It is now housed at the U.S. Library of Congress Prints and Photographs Division in Washington, D.C.

Page 26: A photographer at the Geo. R. Lawrence Company photographed this image of the Chicago stockyards in 1900. This image is housed at the U.S. Library of Congress in Washington, D.C.

Index

About the Author

Aileen Gallagher is a private investigator of corporations and a freelance writer. Her work has appeared in *The New York Law Journal*, *The National Law Journal*, and on Web sites such as *TheStreet.com* and *Blacktable.com*. She has written three other books for the Rosen Publishing Group: *Walter Payton*, *Prince Henry the Navigator*, and *The Japanese Red Army*. She lives in New York City.